HOW TO LIVE ON
BREAD AND MUSIC

Winner of the 2009 JAMES LAUGHLIN AWARD
of the ACADEMY OF AMERICAN POETS

The James Laughlin Award is given to commend and support a poet's second book. It is the only second-book award for poetry in the United States.

Offered since 1954, the award was endowed in 1995 by a gift to the Academy from the Drue Heinz Trust. It is named for the poet and publisher James Laughlin, who founded New Directions Publishing Corp.

JUDGES FOR 2009
Robin Becker
Bob Hicok
Afaa Michael Weaver

Also by Jennifer K. Sweeney

Salt Memory, 2006

HOW TO LIVE ON
BREAD AND MUSIC

JENNIFER K. SWEENEY

PERUGIA PRESS
FLORENCE, MASSACHUSETTS
2009

Perugia Press extends deeply felt thanks to the many individuals whose generosity made the publication of *How to Live on Bread and Music* possible. Perugia Press is a tax-exempt, nonprofit 501(c)(3) corporation publishing first and second books of poetry by women. To make a tax-deductible donation, please contact us directly or visit our Web site.

Cover art is "Angels in Procession," intaglio and aquatint, by Richard Kochanek. See www.kochanek-art.com.

Author photo by Chad Sweeney.

Book Design by Jeff Potter and Susan Kan.

"The Listeners" contains published song lyrics (set off in italics) by: Joan Armatrading, Joan Baez, Solomon Burke, Eva Cassidy, Bob Dylan, Peter Gabriel, Ted Hawkins, Janis Ian, Antonio Carlos Jobim, Joni Mitchell, Van Morrison, Simon and Garfunkel, and Neil Young.

Library of Congress Cataloging-in-Publication Data

Sweeney, Jennifer K. (Jennifer Kochanek)

How to live on bread and music / Jennifer K. Sweeney.

p. cm.

ISBN 978-0-9794582-2-4 (alk. paper)

I. Title.

PS3619.W4426H69 2009

811'.6--dc22

2009014817

Perugia Press

P.O. Box 60364

Florence, MA 01062

info@perugiapress.com

http://www.perugiapress.com

for Chad
and for Mom, Dad, Kathie and Chris

CONTENTS

Nocturne 3

ONE

The Twin 7
I Am Myself Three Selves at Least 9
Adolescence 10
The Three Sisters 12
The Skaters 14
The Silence of Girls 15
Comfort 17
Ballad for the Daily Condition 18
How to Make a Game of Waiting 20
33 Umbrellas 21
How to Live on Bread and Music 22

TWO

The Listeners 25

THREE

Weathering 37
History of Glass 38
Requiem for America 40
How to Make Armor 41
5 O'Clock Poem 42
In Some Forests 44
The Flood 45
How to Feed an Orchid 46
Devotion 47

At 30,000 Feet, Even the Gods Seem Smaller 49

Death Valley 50

How to Uproot a Tree 51

Fragments for the End of the Year 52

FOUR

The Arcata and Mad River Railroad 57

FIVE

In Flight 65

White Shadow 66

Beneath Ice Dunes 68

The Earth Repeats and We Follow 70

How to Grow a Mushroom 71

Erie Central Station 72

How to Tune a Xylophone 73

Yesterday We Watched the Spider Spin 74

In Praise and Apology 76

Today's Lesson: Landscapes 78

Birds of America 79

What Call 81

Presence 82

Song for a White Balloon 83

HOW TO LIVE ON
BREAD AND MUSIC

NOCTURNE

There is a blue city in mind
constructed slantways

along a rippling canal,
clean and unpeopled but for a musician

who plays a harp without strings.
The city has one chair

where he sits by the broad strokes of water.
A lone streetlamp tends

its blue arc of light.
A Persian door. A zeppelin sky.

The world filters through
his empty frame as he plucks the air.

Maybe you hear a song or maybe you don't.
That is the choice we are always making.

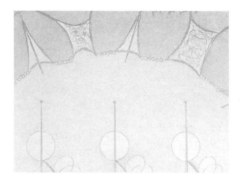

ONE

THE TWIN

To be doubled
as in greater than

$$I + I$$

zygote pair
self swimming the pool of self

or is it halved
as a cleaved grapefruit?

In school, you write him
as your brother,
this lost other
who drank sap with you
in the early dark.

Little Gemini: friend.

Who knows what we are made of?
She of he, I of you
viscous   gloss   confluence
see-through bodies at the rim of time.

To have felt death before sun or word
slippage of the heart-strum,
unbraiding boy.

When the cord was tied
like a slipknot on your belly,
you were both then

dark messenger   gold bread.

You had been with him and made each other,
you already knew *witness   leave   give*
and yet, sister—
you came like a searchlight.

I AM MYSELF THREE SELVES AT LEAST

I am myself three selves at least,
the one who sweeps the brittle
bees, who saves the broken plates

and bowls, who counts to ten,
who tends the shoals,
who steeps the morning's Assam leaves

and when day is wrung
tightens clock springs.
And yes, the one who sat through youth

quiet as a tea stain, whose hand
went up and knees went down,
whose party dresses soaked with rain,

who dug up bones
of snakes and mice
and stashed them inside baby jars—

who did not eat,
but did not starve.
And the self who twists the fallen

dogwood sticks into her hair,
who knows the trick of grief
is there is nothing such as sin

and neither good to part
the air, whom autumn claims
skin by skin.

ADOLESCENCE

1.

In the scoliosis clinic, I waited in a room of skeletons
while men reshaped the architecture of my sister,
spongy discs stacked in S-curves
like haunted seahorses, undulant when I shifted
a protuberance side to side in my thumb
and forefinger and the reticulated whip
rippled to the tailbone.
From the cold gleam of chrome rooms,
girls who were apprenticing to be women
emerged with fallen eyes, torsos fitted
in white plastic bodices like armor.
Cage around cage around echo chamber of heart,
tapered fingers at the hips,
sharp rise of iliac points
directing their sway toward revolving doors.
I stared at the skeletons, at the girls,
at the scooped moon of the pelvis into which
the thighbones fasten like sanded doorknobs.

2.

At 22, I accepted a job teaching junior high.
Not far enough away from the hollow years
of my own shifting body, the seventh and eighth-grade girls,
slight and doe-sprung, drifted down wide industrial
hallways, bones jutting sideways from their skin.
One girl chose my second-story classroom
from where we'd see her fall past the window,
gathered below for the after-school meeting.
She pulled back my chair, tucked her backpack
neatly under my metal desk,
opened the window and let go.
Below, a flash of brown hair, slim form like a sail,
then an anchor, heavy in the grass.
Her silhouette shuddered as we ran.
Don't move! we shouted, but she was already
standing up, walking away into dusk,
not a bone out of place, walking
like a girl who's thrown her body
to the wolves and comes back whole.

THE THREE SISTERS

How many times have I peered into
the sloop and slag of childhood
as if shaking up a snow globe
to watch the three sheaths of our bodies
raised to the world.
Sensitive triad, we were inventors of democracy.
Anything meant for two, we fractioned into thirds:
waiting for a procession of three wishbones
on the windowsill before allowing
the clean snap of chance
and the careful casting and recasting as we acted
our favorite skit, where the woman
tells the waiter she's found a fly in her soup.
Though our three pairs of horn glasses
mingled on the dresser, I'll never see
the world as you did:
second sister, quiet diplomat,
who acquiesced to all my pocket fancies,
slept with me in the walk-in closet,
snacks cached in our sleeping bags,
and pretended our airport reunion
running from opposite sides of the house;
first sister, soothsayer, who faced
into the future like the woman
on the prow of a ship.
When I see a trio of girls
in the Italian restaurant
portioning out plates of pasta
or at the bar mitzvah where the daughters
line up like nesting dolls,
I return to our mythic beginnings.

Those evenings we survived the steely timbre
of a thundershower under the dining table
rigging the storm into story
and afterward, we ran outside in our nightgowns
sweeping across the green-black of the lawn
like ghosts or promises
and pretended the lightning chose us,
changed our chiffon bodies into statue
to be found years later as legend.
Three stone girls under live oaks
who never grew old.

THE SKATERS

They were not actual boots with laces
that crisscrossed our ankles
but a tinny retractable heel-toe
we slid to hug our feet and buckled in place,
and the ice was not an actual rink
but a happenstance of ice,
marshy patch outside the firehouse,
surface deckled by frozen weeds and silt deposits
that caught in our glide.
My sister and I queened the makeshift rink
scrawling circles in the whitewash afternoon,
blades like dull steak knives.
Though we knew ground was inches beneath,
the day the ice cracked under my skates
as if hammered,
her motherly arm wrenched me away,
eyes lit with the recklessness of protection.
Don't tell, she demanded, *this is just between us,*
and in that look we survived something as real as death.

THE SILENCE OF GIRLS

They are not the freshly brushed
or first-musk-behind-ear girls,
not wrapped in the latest sashay and sequin of a shirt.
They are as invisible as the inside of a locker

amidst the swarm of strut-walks
and octave-dropping voices.
This one is hunkered behind a pinched mask,
living off her defenses.

Another uses her shoulders as a cape
pulled up and over her chest
so her blade bones grow rounded as shell.
How the body becomes artifice, accomplice, artillery.

The one in the corner desk wraps in shirt layers,
to hide the film of struggle and dirt she can't scrub
because the water's shut off again.
And the patient one with the Madonna eyes—

mother to her sister—
she invents magic for her in a house of ice,
unfurls it by handfuls
so the little one will never be without glimmer.

The girls carry their mothers in their bodies,
the facades and the truths of them.
They have seen the side of death that is living
through the slow clock of misery.

Their bodies are filled with pockets,

eyes raw with secrets.
They carry their mothers
because their mothers are broken.

COMFORT

Suppose your mother had thorns
which she hid under baggy dresses
and you were just a child.
Would that explain the river between you?

Suppose during your birthday toast
there was a goldfish in your wine glass.
Would it be auspicious or foreboding?
And suppose tenderness is only a small thing

you could give, simple as a peppermint.
Would you wake with the dread you've felt for years?
Or would you remember to feed the lilies
because you're human and they are alive?

BALLAD FOR THE DAILY CONDITION

That mostly we do our living in houses,
rooms inside houses within rows of houses
and everyone is a supporting character in the story
of your life and the story is an unevenly written mystery
with unearned existential leanings,
dreams clinging to you until dinnertime
eclipses the afternoon.

That you could be in the house and someone
could crawl through the bathroom window
while you're scrubbing pots in the kitchen
and the man who leaves only a footprint on the sink
seems to you afterward not a real man,
your wallet warm against his chest
charged with adrenaline, your name
etching its letters in his mind.

That we hurry the days toward an astral future
when there is nothing left to be done.

That we leave our houses
and rub up in subway turnstiles
where phantom hands slide into pockets deep with regret
and you see yourself in the train window
mirrored by the dark tunnel,
see it as you've never seen it before,
fluorescent and sad, and you wonder
if you've always looked sad on trains.

That people tell you things you can't dismiss—
the woman who said that every emotion

is at least two emotions
like this accidental defeat laced with intrigue
and it seems the train is traveling away from you.

That we leave ourselves in places like you have left
yourself on the other side of the bay
and the passage is emptying you until
your body knows what the sea knows
is just matter   *mater   mother.*

That the circuitry of our brains runs amok in the night.
For months now the car crashes and you are pregnant
or you are locked in the library and pregnant
or the man kidnaps you and you tell him you're pregnant,
beg him let you go and he leaves you
at the midnight estuary on the condition
you give him your shoes.
Feeling across the breakers and rocks with cut feet,
your body knows to slip into the shallows
and you ride on the backs of seals
toward the pull of empty ships named after women
and there are everywhere seals,
your soles sting with salt
and you wake with their skin cool on your belly.

That we wake all of us in beds in rooms in houses
to reconstruct the familiar.
The train surfaces to light and everyone sways like kelp.
To cross over is no small thing
but still we do it daily, wordless, with eyes half-shut.

HOW TO MAKE A GAME OF WAITING

This is a capsized game
and there is no display of aces at the end.
Buy a rare and expensive plant that never blooms.
Rearrange your books by the color of the spines.
Bury all your keys that don't unlock anything.
These are not rules but merely suggestions
of what has worked for others.
For instance, the man who painted landscapes
on his daughter's sheet music.
Put a big rock on your desk.
Do not name the rock.
Take the numbers off the clock and mail them
to your creditors.
Stitch the hours onto a kite.
Every night, ask until you can hear what replies.

33 UMBRELLAS

In your sleep
the year advanced.
Perhaps in a Japanese rainstorm

33 umbrellas opened at precisely
the same moment—
a ballooning

then a click—
and you were allowed further.
Go with your blue apples

falling from the night-trees.
Go with your muddled
light.

Carve impossible faces
in the pumpkin.
Scoop a net of seeds—

one for the trouble you've caused,
the rest for the trouble
you wish you caused.

The skeletons wear marigolds
for eyes.
They let you pass,

lantern-hearted, happy.

HOW TO LIVE ON BREAD AND MUSIC

You need not confront the storm
though it comes with its guillotine
of wind and arrows of ice.
Let it come.
Take the wheat in your sage-rubbed hands
and pull out the dull chords.
Fold in Ravel. Hazelnuts.
Fold in the fury,
quarter notes rising from the grain.
These are your hands weighing the earth,
alchemy of salt and scale,
hum of clove bud.
Into the fire your life goes
to work its slow magic
and the song is the yeast
when the body wants
and it wants   fills   empties
as the day   fills   empties.
Song of milk glass.
Song of chaff.
That the thing delivers itself whole
like a blessing.
Feed the animal those brown fields.
Feed the rest of the body any tune,
any note will do.

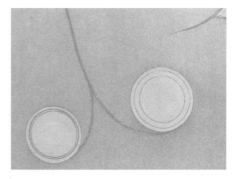

TWO

THE LISTENERS

When darkness rolled in,
my father turned off all the lights

and listened to record albums.
Dylan, Beethoven, Madonna:

a palette that exceeded range.
He'd rush out to us begging someone

to hear what he'd just heard.
Songs of easy chairs, volume and despair,

of eyes closed, deep winter playing the bones.

⁓

tracing circles with my body in the air
a-spin   adrift

if a tree could record a year on a circumference of sap
what multifold was my life being etched on?

ink-drained pen   shucked seed pod   a radial gesture

⁓

That's the trick of listening, he said,
lovingly setting the latest LP
on the polished phonograph.

To find the song that is autobiographical.

~

orchestra in the rift
labyrinthine platter held to the light
a black gleam of simple patterns

~

I'd sit between the six foot speakers,
ache of my adolescence

and his adulthood
soothed by those vinyl voices

surging from the Magnaplanes
in a shared and private anthem.

Lights out, I listened and swayed,
trying to feel what saved him.

Joni Mitchell and Joan Baez
welling up day-feelings, crooning them away.

I was practicing for angst,
some kind of *turbulent indigo.*

~

sail on silver girl

how to make a melody from a needle
how to hide my gravelly voice in a hair's width

the song is in the crack

    what is a crack if not empty space?
    what is a song if not beautiful time
    portioned aside
    by vagabond saints?

                    echoes in the well of silence

    ⁓

to make the night whorl
like a great silver wheel
captive on the carousel of time

    ⁓

Perhaps every groove contained
a stashed eight-count
that could be coaxed into audio
by a drag of needle
or you could be consumed
by a crack of parched earth
and live there like the Jackson 5

condensed to a strand.

I, scientist of not-much-data,
tried to unearth other storehouses of song
playing a dinner plate on my suitcase gramophone.

No ceramic blue cadence
or homage to leftovers
but a haphazard scratchling.

—

oh fishbowl world I have only faith in the miniscule

—

I did leave my *Saturday Night Fever* album
on the July patio
where the vinyl melted to a molten pliant
and I pressed my fingerprints in
but they would not sing.

—

before I knew that magic
is just not understanding how the world works

~

The music teacher told her third graders
if you played "Strawberry Fields Forever" backwards
it would sing *John is dead.*
The children imagined her hand
steering the record counterclockwise
like witchcraft
revealing the secret warped message.
They were shown scratchy movies
on reel-to-reels that ticked like metronomes
from the back of the classroom.
After the credits rolled, the reels rewound.
Flowers sealed up, musicians laid their instruments
in their laps and the paper factory returned
its reams to the trees.

~

Two brothers in Australia devoted their lives
to perfecting the art of playing a record.
Their turntable was a bed of thick felt over glass,
the needle, platinum sharpened to an eyelash
then wrapped in cat intestines
so that as it released from its berth
and lowered to vinyl,
there was only a shock
of friction light as a kiss
along each micro-crevice.

They had made less than a hundred of them
and you had to write to these brothers
to prove your devotion.
The day #38 arrived at our house,
my father unpacked the turntable
and as the needle barely skimmed,
Donna Summer sang a note so perfect
it was turquoise.

~

you could live in that landscape of sound
I saw him do it
quiet nights of quiet stars
calibrating the hours in *diamonds and rust*
troubled water
and a bridge to take him over

~

climb the mountain at noon
perch on rock with aerial view
recess at the Catholic school
the girls make rows on blacktop
when the whistle blows
they lift hula hoops to their waists and twirl
plaid skirts swish silently
perpetual, hypnotic
going round and round in the circle game

the b sides gauge our remnants
patient hourglass
by which a body creaks open
floods with sound
waves
if we were under
water
we would be surrounded
volume up   shake the house
because this is the way through the duration
because I want to see you dance again
on this harvest moon

then there was the summer I was phantom-hearted
spent the heat in my sister's walk-in closet
weepy and love-broke
organizing my father's record collection on Ikea shelves
for a competitive wage

sleeving multiple Dylans into their onion-skin negligees
repeating the songs I could disappear inside of

I was a liqui-solo
unalphabetized wind
quiet phone

at night we sat in the debris
lights out and the speakers
mathematically equidistant
from the center of the room

so when Van spoke
   take me back take me way way back down Hyndforth Street

his dry creek bed voice entered our ears
like the secret of the past

and perhaps we understood its rope-holds
and listened over and over
so as to pull up on that bittersweetness

give me more of what I am consumed with but can't remember

   play someone else's life backwards tonight

—

I really don't know life at all
this train still runs
not dark yet
as long as I can see the light
a change is gonna come

—

When the compact disc came
the brothers in Australia knew
time was opening to swallow an era
and they wanted to depart with it.
Like going down on the ship they built,
they wrote a farewell letter to the owners—
a handful all over the world—
of their famous turntable
and committed dual suicide.

—

river oh river   river running deep
need grief anthems
to pour halved dreams
down to zero
some moonbit night
oh had I a golden thread
after the last note
scratchy silence   insert coda
play over
another revolution in the void
until the airlifted key
until the inner applause of the heart
and still I'd be on my knees
I'd still be on my knees

—

So the years spin by and I too
listen with my eyes closed,

work-skin empties of earthly mass
and the lyric drifts in like a marbled sky.

Song of goldfinch and blue glass.
A song to pass the midnight eternal.

—

another catalogue of nightfalls
he sees life from *both sides now*

the moon a phantom rose
come in from the cold
steal an hour of gold-song-round

while the leaves, snow, fire
while the lightning harasses the sky
the surface breaks, while the mistakes
while the deer rush the yard

come sweet flight of breath
we can't return
the listener is twice-lived

gather the cupped self
scatter time

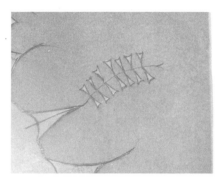

THREE

WEATHERING

After the San Bruno fire

Our new house faced the panorama
of a mountain burnished
to amber stubble by wildfire.

At dusk the sky lowered a spectrum of whites
and rested atop it like thickset netting,
rows of rooftops dwarfish under the fog.

Much of weathering is erasure,
the daily words disintegrating
in the mouth each night to mist.

What to say after the earth opened
its fault line and stole some hillside
before seaming itself back together?

It's been three years.
The beginnings of trees are drafting
the mountains green this spring.

I'm still silenced by that floodplain of fog
obscuring the life
and death of a city each evening,

and how little I know
about anything.
Just today I opened a brand new book

and there in the runnel
of the still-stiff spine,
a single silver hair.

HISTORY OF GLASS

I don't have to remind you of destruction
or how far away from origins
we travel each day,
but consider the prismatic faith
that led the first Iraqi to alchemize
an ashy sand in mantle-heat,
leaden rod dripping with—
what to call it?—
not sand nor fire,
but honey cooled to stone:
glass.

Consider the weight
of that glass bead in his palm,
the moment when only he
understood what he'd made.

Centuries later an Egyptian artisan
poured the iridescent lava into molds.
Think symmetry, cascade, gradation.
Think juice glass, vase.
Swirled with ochre, cobalt and haloed
of its own inner beam.
Mixed with uranium, it glowed the eerie citron
of beetle-swarms in black light.

Follow that molten glass to Rome
where it became blown breath,
a pipe offered to the fire.
How intimate as the crafter gathered
the air in his lungs and sent it

fluted, dragon-like toward what matter
‘   was rapidly going solid, a single exhale—
to expire—small death, blown bowl.

REQUIEM FOR AMERICA

It was not about sadness
though the magnolia
turned while we slept

and we could not find
the iron map of stars.
Sadness would have been a consolation

for that saw-toothed hollow,
would have indicated joy,
but the heart carried

no such sailboat
and we rowed across static.
This was about the first

breath held back,
small death
of instinct,

and when the last
violin was pure
friction

we had only
a few moments
to choose.

HOW TO MAKE ARMOR

Wear your bones like cold-rolled
steel, skin hammered
in brigandine sheets.
Pound leather and shadow
to a stiff segmentata.

Be corset-pinched.

Clad in devices,
night will rise like a wound,
duty bronzed to paldrons
hulking your shoulders.

When your bad decisions are fused
with chain mail and you're dueling
in the silence of thieves,
go at the world in stone.

Fear is a long-revered tradition.

In the carbon-dark, language
is harnessed in its helm
as "order" from the Latin *ordo*
means *closed circle.*

Be plate-sealed,
protected as a priest's halberd
wielding against a cauldron
of medicine.

Or lie naked in the dandelions,
pained with sensation.

5 O'CLOCK POEM

Descending the gray nudge of Market Street
    I am heavy in my shoes,
        a little sack-bent.

The dryness in my throat
    is familiar but not comfortable,
        my body is familiar but not comfortable.

Most openings are too small to enter,
    but upstream and tired, I fall in
        achy stone of me exploding like a rose,

some slat of light, some pod of tenderness.
    People look almost real
        swaying toward the charcoal night into streetcars.

The train is always approaching always pulling out.
    What I mean to say is we live in the illusion
        of beginnings and endings.

Above ground the trucks are coming
    in a flow of red-turning lights.
        By a stream in a life that is not mine

a salmon thrusts the silver
    glint of its body
        up a shallow stream that is pushing it—

can you feel it pushing you?—
    backwards.
        And what if it gave in

let the exhausted muscle of its being
      ride the way-down current.
           All these people how hungry they look

and not nearly as guilty as they feel
      shuffling onto the silverlit train cars
           by ones

as something
      they have been waiting for
           has come to take them home.

IN SOME FORESTS

it is always dark and so night is
a matter of perception.

Dark as when a door is about to close
but does not

and a careful emptiness
is allowed.

Indifference deafens.
Questions can be left behind.

The Zen-eyes of the eagle
care nothing for this moment

as if seeing were a little theft.
Come, come beckons the skipper of the heart.

Who isn't waiting to be filled?
By any creek shade or mock sun.

By the inky green that is greener in here
scrubbed and newly made.

Every year a tree creates
absolutely from scratch

99% of its living parts.
Oh brittle deadwood. Oh bones.

THE FLOOD

There are entire cities in China
emptied of their people

and flooded with bright water
that reflects common stars

as the rooftops sleep below.
By day, tourists lower their pale

bodies beneath the surface
to see the ruins iridesce

with fish.
A premeditated Atlantis

of inroads and cabins.
A schoolhouse filled with rain.

Families dive for the illusion of discovery:
four-post bed,

Buddha too heavy to carry out.
A woman parts the deep

with her hands
as if drawing back curtains,

pauses at her own reflection
on a cracked mirror.

Her divided blue face,
languid hair.

HOW TO FEED AN ORCHID

Clarify the relationship.
It is you being fed and the orchid
who spoons blossoms in your mouth.

Find an east-facing room
quiet as a theatre of monks
watching a woman cross the stage.

Do not involve your own thirst when watering.
Incidental light is preferable to any replica of sun.
Stone, wood, marl or coconut husk
provide anchorage and let it be.

Like your thoughts without television,
the columns will harness the underestimated air
into calyx and corolla.

Urn-shaped or lyrate, barbate or ephemeral,
to nourish the orchid,
maintain a spirit of delicacy
with your dearest.

For the careful rosette and trinity of petals,
it bears the common name of "nun."
But look at its center—
sheathed, gaping, labiate—

no less a woman.

DEVOTION

In a buttoned cardigan and pressed shift,
she leans solemnly against the white porch
column like she has found something
strong enough to bear her grief,
eyes pointed heavily outside the frame.
Perhaps everyone has a photo like this
where the possibility that anything can happen
has just dervished away.
Soon she will marry an Italian man.
He will invent useful things
like the first plastic soda bottle
and a version of her life.
He will ask for a son
and she will name five daughters.
He will build a house to hold their lives,
and that house will be the only one
that could tell the story without vaulted
chests and trapdoors.
She will make the egg noodles each week
out of nothing special,
turning dough in the hand crank
to ribbons the color of old letters.
They will break after they air dry
so she will slide tissue paper under and lower
the cradle into department store shirt boxes.
The daughters will have daughters who will
eat those noodles, dry and chewy
as teething crackers. A shirt box
atop their refrigerator will remind
the girls that devotion is a wheel
turning in ordinary light.

When her husband dies, one granddaughter
will ask at the wake
Grandma, would you like some pasta?
and she will answer squarely
No, I never liked Italian food.

AT 30,000 FEET,
EVEN THE GODS SEEM SMALLER

The Sierra Nevada are crumpled in sun-burnt ridges and gullies
as the skin of the Italian grandfather

we've just buried
might have looked under the magnifying glass

Grandma uses to read the newspaper.
Our patterns of weathering are, mathematically speaking, similar—

the way the earth is 75% saltwater and 25% land mass
and we are 75% saltwater and 25% tissue mass,

small worlds of us divinely aging
as storms trench the flatirons,

rain striates maple bark
and the moth-etchings of habit and wind score our faces.

But the surfaces only tell us time has been here.
If one could spread out the duration of love

between a daughter and a father across glass fields,
study the fissures,

undershadow of mesa—
who knows if it would change silence.

Here on the other side of our lives
we are much too far away.

DEATH VALLEY

The desert is a woman with no ideas—

an unfurrowed plain,

a sanded-down noon.

It's where I go when the briar rose

has swallowed the fence

and it's thickening toward the door.

Oh life with your falling open,

April is eating itself alive

and I can hear the splitting of the dahlias

when I sleep.

A ghost wind stirs in the canyon walls.

The stone in me rests.

As night dims the sky, the broken

sunset   pivots

on the wings of a flock

and they carry it away.

HOW TO UPROOT A TREE

Stupidity helps.
Naiveté that your hands will undo
what does perfectly without you.
My husband and I made the decision
not to stop until the task was done,
the small anemic tree made room
for something prettier.
We'd pulled before, pale hand over wide hand,
a marriage of pulling toward us what we wanted,
pushing away what we did not.
We had a shovel which was mostly for show.
It was mostly our fingers tunneling the dirt
toward a tangle of false beginnings.
The roots were branched and bearded,
some had spurs
and one of them was wholly reptilian.
They had been where we had not
and held a knit gravity
that was not in their will to let go.
We bent the trunk to the ground and sat on it,
twisted from all angles.
How like ropes it was,
the sickly thing asserting its will
only now at the end,
blind but beyond
the idea of leaving the earth.

FRAGMENTS FOR THE END
OF THE YEAR

On average, odd years have been the best for me.

I'm at a point where everyone I meet looks like a version
of someone I already know.

Without fail, fall makes me nostalgic for things I've never experienced.

The sky is molting. I don't know
if this is global warming or if the atmosphere is reconfiguring
itself to accommodate all the new bright suffering.

I am struck by an overwhelming need to go to Iceland.

Despite all awful variables, we are still full of ideas
as possible as unsexed fruit.

I was terribly sorry to be the one to explain to the first graders
the connection between the sunset and pollution.

On Venus you and I are not even a year old.

Then there were two skies.
The one we fly through and the one
we bury ourselves in.

I appreciate my wide beveled spatula which fulfills
the moment I realized I would grow up and own such things.

I am glad I do not yet want sexy bathroom accessories.

Such things.

In the story we were together every time.

On his wedding day, the stone in his chest
not fully melted but enough.

Sometimes I feel like there are birds flying out of me.

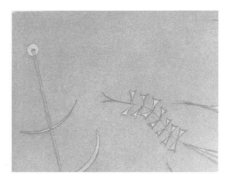

FOUR

THE ARCATA AND
MAD RIVER RAILROAD

i.

by the slow burn
of summer
I walk the old railroad tracks
no wind through rattle
snake grass
the flax
is a yellow field
of arrows

all sound draws down
monotone buzz
of bugs
skittering gravel
my steps measure out
in rungs

ii.

left alone the railroad
has buried itself
in wildflowers
is graveyard
and the granite buckling
of memory

july is a kind of amnesia

my grandfather became like that too
his mind
overgrown and deserted
the scrapbook past
screeched by invisibly
how he insisted
how we could not see it

iii.

thorned heat prods
at vulnerability
neck and knee
the buried splinter
of desire

something lost
fallen precisely
upon tracks
something sacrificed
placed oh so carefully
welded down
by the hot iron of motion

array of coins
bottle caps
gold cross
a spoon
soldier's brassy button
a child's ring
pocket knife
harmonica

iv.

palette of late-summer
slow flush of green
ripeness recedes into the gold
that dead things are

so it is death then—
the subtle note repeating across the meadow
which I accept as beauty

spring's yarrow
now an orchestra
of brittle flutes
the one numinous breath plays
chorus of the separate made whole

v.

At the ramshackle depot
an odd museum of things
driven down by iron stakes:

Pacific Rail timetable   Arcata departs 8:00 A.M.

            expired license   a *William T*

                        pocket journal

dining car menu
                    coffee 10 cents

        laminated map of Northern California

how our things speak for us   and what you've left behind

                (tree house, sister, tradition, ambition)

is continually arriving as it is found and found and found

vi.

as the tracks fork
out of town
a cluster of
other things
people wanted nailed down

framed black-and-white photo of a girl
King James Bible
wristwatch
Nixon political button
divorce papers

and the need itself to be remembered
rumbling beneath the rails

vii.

when I am sun-tired I lie down
pretend I am tied or
have caught my pants on the rail

the Starlight Express
thundering its storm whistle
and just as the first wheels keen my shoulders

I reel onto the grainy bank
my life flashing in a dust devil
open my eyes to the tessellation of clouds

which look hallowed
open my eyes to a bird
a bird which is always a departure

FIVE

IN FLIGHT

The Himalayan legend says
there are beautiful white birds
that live completely in flight.
They are born in the air,

must learn to fly before falling
and die also in their flying.
Maybe you have been born
into such a life

with the bottom dropping out.
Maybe gravity is claiming you
and you feel
ghost-scripted.

For the one who lives inside the fall,
the sky beneath the sky of all.

WHITE SHADOW

I sweep leaves from my porch deck
but against the grain of the wood
their shapes remain

like stuck shadows or slow
obscura prints.
Elegant stars of Japanese maple,

princess flowers echoed in ovular chevrons.
I knew a photographer
who trapped the moon

using photosynthesis paper
and plates of glass.
After many nights the thin curve

appeared on black film
like true evidence—
shape shadow form fade.

He wrapped gelatin paper
around a redwood trunk during El Niño
and the forty-day rain dripped

a striated portrait of falling,
pastel egoless art.
If I could exchange the personal landfill

of my thirty-five years
for a slow flux image
of my sleeping posture, I would.

But I am bound to a life of tidying—
folding grocery sacks, squirting
dish soap, dismantling vacuum bags

that carry residue of my days
in their poundage of hair and body ash.
My best apology is in seeing:

perfection of spores under the sword fern,
jasmine vine wound to a spring-loaded curl.
Orchid,

I watch you again,
choosing for the second winter
to send up impossible blooms

in the freezing yard.
White shadow against the bare fence,
your stalks bow.

BENEATH ICE DUNES

In memory of Charles Darling

Spring comes early and stays
long enough for the plum blossoms
to believe it.

Not a gradual blooming but
pink, suddenly—
dotting cement and grass the same.

Is it too much to ask that it not leave?
Fragrance, the belled
sunlight, your remission.

When I was eighteen I stood
beneath plum, cherry
waiting for a foreign wind

to blow a confetti of departure
and thought
this is happiness I have felt it.

A door closes and the cold
returns, asking more of the world
than the world can give.

I think of chanterelles calcified
beneath snow-capped headlands,
bearded irises waiting

under lids of ice,
monarchs huddled
in tree hollows.

Once you wrote to me in a poem:
If I died like that beneath ice dunes or anywhere
away from home, would my soul know where to go?

The plum tree shivers in the frost,
slender branches sprouting
in spite of silence.

THE EARTH REPEATS
AND WE FOLLOW

the earth repeats itself
                       so tiny in our houses
a forest fills with questions
                       one who never leaves, cannot return
to walk with the urgency of bees
                       when I say she I mean mother
looking for a new home
                       a language of silences
over moss creeks, alyssum
                       if words do not fall, they are buried
trees are governed by space and light
                       a body wraps in maps
growth is a fracturing
                       I become what I cannot say
see the cypress reclined on the hill
                       the earth repeats
and we follow
                       light hardens into leaves

HOW TO GROW A MUSHROOM

You're going to need soil and not out of the bag
but a vegetal mud dampened by umbrella fern,
a little scat, silt, shreds of orange peel
for the proper asexual cavedom.

Don't simulate the rain with a leaky bucket.
Don't sculpt a village out of sediment and moss.
Let religion recede.
Think paisley fish breathing eucalyptus.

Eat Hog Island oysters on the half-shell three times a week.
Let light fracture.
A glob of witch's butter on a nearby fringe cup
is a sign of good luck.

Think oxide strata and mica subduction.
Out of tallow seepage,
a tweedy stump,
a zinc-capped nudge.

Let night harvest the camphor moon.
Chanterelle or cowboy's handkerchief,
a cosmology of debris
in the unlikely cadence of noon.

ERIE CENTRAL STATION

It was theatrical once,
the arrivals and departures,
cathedral ceilings, opera windows
and burgundy velvet couches.
At 3 A.M. a bent-back man
crawls out from the dark with a skeleton key
to unlock Erie Central Station
and the people, a handful each night,
emerge from snow drifts,
their facades stiff with wakefulness,
but otherwise languid as flashbacks.
Against the peeling walls the businessmen
lean like a pack of trench coat angels,
and under the unlit chandelier,
two college girls who've nowhere to go.
I'd like to think every night contains a fissure
where a couple of strangers are cast
in the grand light of an approaching train,
not the station where the train stops
but the station where the station stops,
and they choose something for which
they are completely unprepared.

HOW TO TUNE A XYLOPHONE

Go for a drive and let it sit in the passenger seat.
When the air feels dusty as a roadside chapel,
pull over and start walking.
If you come across train tracks,
lay the xylophone on the rungs
and let the vibrations tune it.
One note is a wasp boring holes in the air.
One note is a bleached newspaper
rattling in the brush.

YESTERDAY WE WATCHED THE SPIDER SPIN

oh my dear it is gone
the night has taken it down

I wipe cobwebs from my eyes
how long have we been sleeping?

there are a thousand ways to falter
but today

let's be impatient with our suffering
the cold knife cuts the apple

with such clarity
and when we see our lives

without scaffolding
we too are that precise

just yesterday we watched the spider
spin its natural math

a home of dust and intention
stretched wide as a flag

across the boxwood
we watched the outer octagon

threading inward
toward the final moment of center

the night is god
is coming again and oh

my dear does the spider mourn
like we do?

our home
is the moment

when we touch
is this waxing toward love

IN PRAISE AND APOLOGY

For the man whose Impala breaks down on the highway mid-lane,
his face wrinkled in agony as he heaves the machine toward gravel.

For grief which slows time and makes everything sad and beautiful—
the children's art hanging crooked in the museum,
a woman carrying a loaf of bread with both hands.

For the Harlem Renaissance painted on an old boot.

For renewal, a woman's vintage slip
stretched around a lampshade like light shining through a body.

For grief which makes details appear to have meaning
as when we bought new koi for our pond
and hoped they would have babies but they didn't.

For the time being.

For beach grass, boxwood, bearded iris, calla lily, yucca, ghost rose.
We make these things grow.
They are of us and we are of them,
but they do not belong to us any more than this house.
Neither my body anymore which I have left across the city
in medical buildings and turrets of wind.

For giving back everything borrowed.

For the Chinese-American teenager
who described herself as a paper daughter.

For the man who wakes from his surgery

and wails into the cold *Am I alive?*

For irony, that writes itself into our lives
making them fictions to us.

For the homeless woman who sang to me at the gas station,
You're just too good to be true, Can't take my eyes off of you,
mottled black arms outstretched to the clouds.

For my students searching in silence
the alley-cracks and gutters for haiku in their composition books.

For the greater strength it takes the woman
who has been pushing an immense rock for years
to walk the opposite direction.

TODAY'S LESSON: LANDSCAPES

The art teacher would have preferred a job at the academy.
Her gaggle of second graders press
the drafting tables with primary colors,
stick figure families and a devotion to rainbows.
Today's lesson: Landscapes.
Many describe a bottom inch of green
with a huddle of daisies, square house,
V of birds and sun in the corner,
rays portrayed by yellow spokes.
We don't draw suns in our pictures.
They swallow hard and knit their brows,
imagining sunless paintings.
It seemed a terrible thing.
When you look at a real landscape,
there is no bright wedge of sun in the corner.
The world doesn't look like that.
She gives them oil pastels and watercolors.
Sun is the light cast on the whole landscape,
dimmer on cloudy days, pinkish at sunset.
She shows them how to blend light into gradients,
how to bend the sky.
The children's landscapes begin to appear holy.
Stick figures and boxy red cars illumined with halos,
airplanes flying through a wash of honey,
curly treetops giving off an aura of gold.
Still, that upper corner beckons to many
and as night pinkens the light over the pentagonal houses,
a few seagulls fly up into the sun's vacancy
bound off-page
in search of a new theory.

BIRDS OF AMERICA

When I let my class of boys read,
they fly to their refuges of lap and word.
Philip heaves a complete hardback of *Calvin and Hobbes*
from under his seat like the Dead Sea Scrolls.
Adam lunges for another volume of *Greek Myths*
and Jack is inaccessible in his Tolstoy-thick *Star Wars Trilogy.*

They select these tomes of escape,
guidebooks for the fourth-grade boy.
In the silence, the dog-eared pages,
stained with snack chip grease and fever,
turn themselves, eyes pouring wide
as only a boy's attention does.
An attention not with one's whole body,
for they have long disconnected from that gravity,
but an attention without the body,
which is, as Daedalus might agree,
a prerequisite for flight.

I may not get them back,
having sent them off to past and future tenses
with no means of retrieval.
Adam tips his red chair over the edge of balance
and it flies him back Icarus-like on his head.
Dazed and open-mouthed, he insists he is fine
and is lost again.

Jordan is most fascinating,
darting to the meager library's reference shelf to retrieve
Birds of America, a blue upholstered birder's bible.
He is the only one who has ever read it

and does so as a sailor reads the sky and all its falling,
methodically, page one to end,
as if the order bears a secret numerology.

Kingfisher   Cinnamon Teal   Rufus-Sided Touhee

After struggling all day to stay focused,
Birds of America is Jordan's anchor,
harvesting his own version of happiness.

When he tells me that 69% of all Great Blue Herons die
in their first year and that someday he might be as tall
as their six-foot wingspan, I remember how one flu-ridden spring
a grayish trench coat swaggered past my city window
like an apparition or codeine side effect
and landed on the neighboring roof peak.

The Great Blue Heron folded into its scythe-like form,
a messenger miles from any marshland
and bearing something I wasn't able to see.

WHAT CALL

My bedroom was the only one in our house that faced east. Overspilling. Absurdly pink. I liked night best because I knew it would come. From the window I listened to the second story of elm trees rustling, wordless, oceanlike. So much of what has soothed me has not been human. I drank in the sound, fantasized about love and death until the 11 o'clock freight train rumbled along the edge of town and how I let myself drift into that funneling. My family claimed I made the train up along with other memories no one had. Hard to know still, which world is more real, doubt or beauty? I had to go with what came every night, what call fogged through the trees to tell me to keep going, that train that only now after retrieving something from my closet late at night, did my father agree was real.

PRESENCE

Maybe it comes when you catch the queen
bee mating in the boxwood

or the afternoon you realize
the rosemary has taken the path.

You wake in moments,
wonder which sprung hour spawned:

when you chose instead to read,
in the dimly haloed dawn.

There is little life
you can fully witness.

Even your own you drift
in and out of seeing.

Nails need trimming again.
Heart, so suddenly tired.

The jacaranda's bloomed, you shout,
to find it's been purple for days

and you are left to uncover
the small actions completed all around you

drenched in quietude,
that have already begun

to wane into some other
push and pulse of form.

SONG FOR A WHITE BALLOON

one simple thing
a weightless note full of rise

form as dependent on breath
breath as dependent on lungfuls of habit and duty

two white balloons behind the bone cage
sea-moons buoyant in the sea-body

on the night of her birthday
a woman dreams of a thousand

white balloons pouring
from the curtains of the sea

everything winterish and beautiful
a thousand billowings

falling as pieces of sky fall
all the time and we do not see them

this is the gravity of happiness
giving breath back

the world is possible
and beyond human

ACKNOWLEDGMENTS

I am grateful to the following periodicals in which these poems first appeared, some in slightly different form or under different titles:

Barrow Street: "In Flight" (as "Still Life with Egg")

Calyx: "At 30,000 Feet, Even the Gods Seems Smaller"; "Song for a White Balloon"

Crab Orchard Review: "The Silence of Girls"

Del Sol Review: "Comfort"; "How to Live on Bread and Music"

DMQ Review: "33 Umbrellas"

Electronic Poetry Review: "How to Make a Game of Waiting"; "What Call"

Eleven Eleven: "Erie Central Station"; "I Am Myself Three Selves at Least"

Gargoyle: "Death Valley"

Hunger Mountain: "The Flood"; "Fragments for the End of the Year"

Main Street Rag: "How to Uproot a Tree"

OCHO: "The Arcata and Mad River Railroad" (as "Other Things People Wanted Nailed Down")

Parthenon West Review: "How to Make Armor"

Phoebe: "5 O'Clock Poem"

Rattle: "Birds of America"

RUNES: "Yesterday We Watched the Spider Spin"

Southern Review: "Ballad for the Daily Condition"

Spoon River Poetry Review: "The Twin"; "White Shadow"

The Pedestal Magazine: "How to Grow a Mushroom"

Water~Stone Review: "Requiem for America"

"In Flight" was chosen as a letterpress broadside at the Kalamazoo Book Arts Center's Poets in Print Series.

For their guidance and attention to these poems, I am indebted to Chad Sweeney, Annie Stenzel, Katherine Case, Patricia Caspers, Janell Moon, Jennifer Arin and Virginia Westover. Special thanks to Susan Kan, Annie Boutelle and Mark Irwin, and to my father for his beautiful art. I am especially grateful to the San Francisco Arts Commission and to Hedgebrook for providing a grant and a residency, respectively, that supported this manuscript.

ABOUT THE AUTHOR

Jennifer K. Sweeney's first book of poems, *Salt Memory,* won the 2006 Main Street Rag Poetry Award. Twice nominated for a Pushcart Prize, her poems have appeared in numerous journals, including *Southern Review, Hunger Mountain, Crab Orchard, Spoon River* and *Passages North* where she won the 2009 Elinor Benedict Poetry Prize. She was awarded a grant from the San Francisco Arts Commission and a residency from Hedgebrook. Sweeney holds an MFA from Vermont College and serves as assistant editor for *DMQ Review.* After living in San Francisco for twelve years, she currently lives in Kalamazoo, Michigan, with her husband, poet Chad Sweeney.

ABOUT PERUGIA PRESS

Perugia Press publishes one collection of poetry each year, by a woman at the beginning of her publishing career. Our mission is to produce beautiful books that interest long-time readers of poetry and welcome those new to poetry. We also aim to celebrate and promote poetry whenever we can, and to keep the cultural discussion of poetry inclusive.

Also from Perugia Press:

- *Two Minutes of Light,* by Nancy K. Pearson
- *Beg No Pardon,* by Lynne Thompson
- *Lamb,* Frannie Lindsay
- *The Disappearing Letters,* Carol Edelstein
- *Kettle Bottom,* Diane Gilliam Fisher
- *Seamless,* Linda Tomol Pennisi
- *Red,* Melanie Braverman
- *A Wound On Stone,* Faye George
- *The Work of Hands,* Catherine Anderson
- *Reach,* Janet E. Aalfs
- *Impulse to Fly,* Almitra David
- *Finding the Bear,* Gail Thomas

This book was typeset in Arno Pro, a type family designed in 2007 by Robert Slimbach for Adobe Systems, Inc.

The type, both beautiful and legible, combines classical letterforms with a warm and graceful calligraphic style.